The
Watchful
Eye

ALSO BY ANNE WATERS GREEN

Minute Men and Women

The Season Lengthens

The Watchful Eye

Selected Poems

ANNE WATERS GREEN

swanhorse

THE WATCHFUL EYE

swanhorse

An Imprint of Monte Ceceri Publishers

Cover design includes elements of "Green Watercolor Eye" by Nika_Akin, "Taiwan Hehuan Mountain" by tingyaoh, and "Sky" by Pexels, courtesy of Pixabay. Interior eye icon by Werayuth Tessrimuange, courtesy of Vecteezy.

Green, Anne Waters, 1941– author
The watchful eye / Anne Waters Green
ISBN: 978-1-949512-24-3 (paperback)
ISBN: 978-1-949512-25-0 (eBook)
1. Poetry. 2. Free verse. 3. Pastoral poetry. 4. South Atlantic States. 5. Feminist poetry. 6. Autobiographical poetry. 7. Art and literature. I. Title

Monte Ceceri Publishers
Savannah, GA
www.swanhorse.com
www.montececeri.com

monte ceceri

For Jim

Contents

1

II

The
Watchful
Eye

Ecstasy

is like that night I drove
three hours
in blinding rain
to keep a date with you,
the torrent intensifying
with each mile
until I reached your house
when it was at its peak.
I stood in your door
soaked to the skin,
water dripping
from my hair into my eyes.
You wrapped me in a towel
warm from the dryer.
I'd waited years for such
a show of love.
Romance is too
weak a word.

Time Suspended

A bald eagle hovers over Osceola Lake
circles, soars, flaps
its mighty wings, not once descends
to snag fish or duck.
A queue of turtles suns unmolested
on a storm-downed tree.
For ten long minutes, we stand and watch,
our walk abandoned.
The eagle prefers coasting thermals
to dining. We choose
gazing upward.

I Did Not Learn the Stars

—For Jim

I never found Orion's Belt
nor dippers, large and small,
but on this mountain the sky
is bigger, blacker; the stars seem
brighter and more numerous
than anywhere
I've been.

And I am more aware.

On this clear night, I follow you into the dark.
A firefly flashes among the trees,
its lamplit tail frantic
beneath the solemn lights above. I think
of summers long ago; a restless girl
chasing lightning bugs. These same stars
shone nameless overhead.

You know the stars, point out Polaris,
show how Big Dipper guides
the watchful eye,
true north.

Gorges State Park, Transylvania County, North Carolina

The trail snakes
     a dense thicket
of tall rhododendron
     whose slender trunks
lean and twist, a maze
     of interlocking webs. Spindly
silhouettes contort

in awkward curtsies
     like barrier
islands' salt-pruned oaks
     forever bowing west,
battered by harsh Atlantic

winds. This highland gorge,
     home to rock walls
     and waterfalls, lies far
from oceanic gales. What force

fashioned this canopy of capricious
     shapes? What hand
     sowed Carolina star moss
and Oconee bell?

GALES

Jesus told Nicodemus the Spirit
wafts as it pleases, just like the wind.

March should be the roaring month,
this year May, consumed with wind.

From my porch, I hear cardinals call,
stare at trees, leaves roiled by wind.

At the beach waves, sun, sand,
my skin tingles, caressed by wind.

The Greeks supposed the universe
was made of water, earth, fire, wind.

In the beginning before first light,
over the dark abyss, a mighty wind.

And I, Anne, whose name means grace,
ponder these forces—Spirit and wind.

Sulphur Springs Loop, Paris Mountain State Park

The trail meanders mountain terrain. Trees felled
by wind or ice, uprooted by rain, lie worn, stripped.
Nubs of former limbs spike out like whittled spears. How

many decades of storms have littered this park built
by men coming of age in the Great Depression? Few
remnants of their work survive but gales' blusters

and sleet's pings have left their marks in ragged shapes,
stark and startling. An oak stands tall, bare. Two forked
limbs stretch heavenward like the *crucifixus dolorosus*

of a dying thief pleading to be remembered. A log, hollow
and decaying, rests beside the path, four openings along
its bole like the holes of that oldest instrument, the flute.

What airs do breezes play passing through those apertures, what
marches blast with summer thunderstorms, what elegies when
winter's snows swirl with only huddling deer to hear?

Screened Porch Afternoon

Sunbeams like strobe-lit
disco steps dance
across a ceiling painted
blue to ward off haints,
reflect tide-tugged
currents in the canal outside.

You, motionless on the dock
in weather-bleached
rocker, long legs stretched out,
arms folded, gray head atilt,
become my father years ago.

I wonder how blue paint
can block the spirit world
if blue skies cannot.

JOY

—After Raymond Carver

Already we've walked the length
of town, visited the Roosevelt Arch,
strolled to where the Gardner empties
into the Yellowstone.
A group in wet suits hauls rubber rafts
to the river, boards, pushes off.
Snowmelt has the water running fast.
My grandson and I watch as they bob
under the bridge, then we scurry to catch
a glimpse on the other side.
Too late.
When we reach the street, I'm panting,
the crafts are out of sight. We meander
back to our motel. It's afternoon,
still hours before time
to meet our group.
The boy sprawls on his bed with a book.
I sit on the porch outside our room.
The June day is cool, a breeze stirs,
the river rushes by, rafts hurdle past.

Joy.
It swells when we least expect it.

Indigo Bunting

A flutter of blue against greens
and browns of the thicket,
you land on the forest floor
feathers swirling like
the bobbing tulle
of a dancer's tutu.
Then in a flash
of blue-black you
fly.

I remain still,
awed by this
gift of grace
on an early
morning
in July.

ALONG THE LAUREL RIVER TRAIL

We hike a path slick with recent rain.
On one side, the river runs and tumbles,
swirls its rocky bed. Opposite, a steep slope
teems green with ferns and moss, flows

wet with frequent waterfalls. Trees, boughs
bare of leaves, trunks embroidered silver
with lichens, hold the banks, some straight,
others storm-bent in ungainly shapes.

Midstream a limbless trunk lies wedged
in the crannies of a boulder, flotsam
of some flood, we guess. A stone urn stands
in a hillside hollow, weather-roughened,

glazed with verdigris. A spout at its base spews water
from the stream above. We wonder why it's there,
laugh when someone says, "It's for the Methodists.
The Baptists get the river." Five merganser ducks

frolic near the far shore. The males' bodies flash
whiter than well-bleached laundry, contrast
their shiny black backs. With their redheaded
girlfriends, they fight their way upstream,
glide down, twirl and pivot in eddies,
swim up, glide down, over and over
and over again.

Migration

These agile acrobats fly up and down, even backward —
bodies, tiny, iridescent and green —
throats ruby red when sun reflects their feathered ascots,
hover over salvia, petunias, thistle to sup.

Bodies, tiny, iridescent and green,
flap their wings fast, creating a hum,
hover over salvia, petunias, thistle to sup.
Native to the Americas.

They flap their wings fast, thus creating a hum,
as they fly at a rapid rate.
Native to the Americas.
Each spring and fall follow their path.

They fly at a rapid rate
from south to north and vice versa,
each spring and fall to follow their path
Five hundred miles over the Gulf without ever making a stop.

SOME WEIGH LESS THAN A PENNY

Tiny flying
gymnasts visit
hundreds of flowers daily
to consume their weight in nectar, always just a single
night away from death.
Fast metabolism drives wings
to beat so   rapidly   they make
a   humming   sound   audible
to human ears.   The name
became   hummingbird.
They play favorites,
pollinate a narrow
spectrum, guard
home territory
with ferocity.
Nature's
reward:
long
life.

Cypress Knees

sprout
in dank silt
encircle ancestor trees, sustain,
anchor, maybe breathe for them
in soft and muddy habitats.

might
I when night,
infirmity, ravages of age
prey, be blessed by such sage
protectors — merited or not.

A Busy Intersection in Savannah

At the corner of Skidaway
    and Eisenhower, a flock
        of ordinary pigeons

congregates on a utility wire
    black silhouettes
        against the sky.

At what must be the faintest
    of signals, they rise and fly
    to land on the car wash

across the street, swing from wash to wire
    and back, gliding like a company

of dancers obeying a master choreographer
    or a congregation of believers moving
    from pew to altar.

Gathering the Flocks

1.
A flock of snow geese
gleans a Louisiana
rice field.

2.
For which of the priest's
flock does the bell
toll?

3.
The bordello's red flocked
wallpaper grows
more tattered
every year.

4.
In fields near Bethlehem,
shepherds watch
over their flocks
by night.

5.
When a coyote nears,
the flock of geese
takes to the sky
in a single fluid
upsweep.

6.
Christmas tree lights glow,
reflect limbs flocked
with artificial snow.

7.
The nouveaux riches
show off the brocade
flocks on their dining
room walls.

8.
A pat of flamingos
is also a flock.

9.
Flocks of tourists crane
their necks to view
the Sistine ceiling.

10.
North to south. South
to north. Flocks fly
a migratory
V.

Loggerhead

She floats on sargassum mats, grows large
in an abundant habitat. Mates.

An inner compass pulls her hundreds
maybe thousands of miles to lay

eggs where she began. In dark she hauls her huge
body across her natal beach, trademark tracks

tendering silent testimony of return. Flippers — graceful
in water, awkward on land — scour a nest

to shelter her clutch. Like a mother who spreads blankets
over sleeping babies, she refills the cavity with sand

before crawling back to sea. Her eggs nest until hatchlings abandon
shells, dig toward shore. Instinct stirs by night.

Moonlight dancing on waves draws a parade
of newborn sea turtles to the deep.

MESS? WHAT MESS?

Outside my window, a plastic pot
hangs from a shepherd's hook,
cradles the bougainvillea
I nursed throughout the winter,

hauled inside on freezing nights,
lugged back out on warmer days,
pruned late in the dormant season
just as my gardening book advised.

Daily I awake, watch, cheer each new sprig,
rejoice as crimson blooms unfold, fume
when a clump of twigs appears, clutters
the bed where my plant is resurrecting.

Where'd that mess come from?

I soon find out. You, Carolina wren,
with those bright white stripes tattooed
along your head, ferry
straw, moss, even cellophane,

make my bougainvillea basket
your building lot, its thorny vine
your landscape, shape a domed abode.
Now at dawn, it's you I long to see.

A WALK AROUND LAKE MAYER

A cormorant suns in a laurel, wings spread
like pannier skirts in a Velasquez portrait,
neck graceful as any Spanish lady's,
a fish held tight in its long, curved bill.

A squadron of keen-eyed pelicans spots
supper beneath the water, circles, dives.
Two men, fishing poles shouldered,
scurry to follow.

An anhinga perches on a stump,
neck stretched, dry wings folded
against its svelte torso, displays
feathers arranged like piano keys.

Hiking Bearwallow in Winter

What path to take?
    Service road
        or steeper trail?

We choose the harder climb.

You let me lead. Otherwise,
    I'd soon be far behind.

The narrow path winds upward
    stone steps at
        the steepest
            places.

The climb: find a spot,
    plant one boot,
        then the other.

Over and over, I haul my body up,
    often using hands,
        even all fours, maybe

grabbing a tree. Locating
    footholds leaves little
        time to look around.

I see only the ground ahead, in places
    wet with melted snow,
        in others, strewn with rocks.

Trying not to stumble, I glimpse only lichen-
    pockmarked trunks. At last we reach
        a grassy bald dotted with boulders.

Reward for the hard climb — a view in three directions —
    over Mount Mitchell, Pisgah, and Hickory Nut Gorge.
        Even with the trees bare of leaves,
            the world below looks green.

MORTALITY

What keeps my heart open
are the trees—live oaks, native
magnolias, palmettos.
Mornings from my screened porch
I gaze beyond beds of hosta,
hydrangea, and ginger into woods.
Like Frost, I think I know
whose woods these are
but no one ever ventures
in from the other side.

I bury compost beneath
leaf mold and Spanish moss.
My eyes view the yellow-green
backlit by sun, the glossy
verdigris of fresh magnolia
leaves, their rust-tinged color
as newness wears away.
I find calm in the still, excitement
when wind ruffles, amazement
that I can neither count nor
label the shades of green.

A nursing home lies past
oak, sweet gum, palmetto.
Sometimes I hear the clank

of a dumpster being emptied.
I know nothing of the souls
who pass their days, weeks,
lives beyond the trees.
Aware of my own years, I
imagine some are younger
than I, others perhaps close
in age to me. I pray they see
the trees' colors, height, shadows,
that their hearts are open too.

THE OLD SMITH PLACE

Jersey, Arkansas

Outside walls of shiplapped
heart pine, a roof of cedar
shingles, brick pier footings,
the house was built to keep

weather out, family safe.
To the woman, it was home
and livelihood. Her husband
had provided well, farmer,

merchant, Justice of the Peace.
When he died, their younger
children still at home, she
earned their bread as

as the village postmistress.
Boxes with glass panes
and combination locks
stretched across her hall.

A window shelf with bell
welcomed folks who walked
right in to collect their mail.
All rang the chime because

no one knew the combinations.
Besides, calling for Miz Jim gave
a chance to swap family news,
hear the latest gossip. Porches

graced both front and back, one
for evening talk when work was done,
dishes washed and dried, the other
for chores, stringing beans, shelling peas.

Large rooms flanked the hall,
on one side her bedroom
where the woman had birthed
babies; on the other, the parlor

where sons and sons-in-law spun
yarns while waiting to be fed
and women gathered afternoons
to stitch on a quilting frame suspended

from hooks screwed in plaster
overhead. In the yard two wells, one
gave sweet drinking water, the other
fit only to douse daylilies, nandina,

black-eyed Susie. Miz Jim's been dead
decades now, the place caved in. Heirs
stripped pine siding from inside walls
to provincialize their fancy homes.

We went one day to take a look, found brick
piers, sunken steps, a few nandinas
in the scraggly yard. And those quilting
hooks still tight in the parlor ceiling.

Reincarnation

—After *Between Earth and Heaven*
  by El Anatsui (2006)

Scraps scavenged

from the dump: whiskey

labels, beer bottle caps,

red, black, gold,

copper-stitched detritus.

Art like the kente

cloth, silk or cotton,

the sculptor's father

weaves back

home in Ghana.

Rippling elegance hung

on museum walls.

Urban Altarpiece

—After *The Voice of the City of New York Interpreted*
by Joseph Stella (1920 – 1922)

Harbors teem in daylight. Tugs guide ships to berths.
Longshoremen heave and grunt as they load and unload
cargo. Foghorn whistles resound for miles. Stella ignores
the bustle. A night sky looms over tanks, piers, ocean.

Weary stevedores
Fall asleep on subways home
Wharf rats claim the port

Taxicabs swerve and honk down Broadway. Tourists
stumble or skip along crowded sidewalks. Trains rumble
underground. Theater marquees shout silently. Neon
bounces off rain slick streets.

Backstage angels pray
Nervous directors fidget
Actors peruse scripts

Modern buildings tower over brownstones. Industry
breathes energy into city air. New York floats above
Manhattan Island like a giant oceangoing vessel cutting
through waves, conquering land and sea. Does the center
panel pay homage or hurl blasphemy to the cross of Christ?

As speculators applaud
Wall Street's rampant greed
Girls toil in sweatshops

New York vibrates, celebrates, dominates. Midtown
north, midtown south, the Big Apple pulses with sound.
Streetcars clang, vendors hawk hot dogs, newsboys
holler "Extra," bands boom Sousa marches, pipe organs
blast and whisper fugues and sonatas.

News—*Hot off the press*
Nineteenth Amendment passes
Women *gain the vote*

The bridge sweeps over the East River, cambered span
soars high above barges, scows and merchant ships.
Borough to borough. Manhattanites promenade on
Coney Island, Brooklynites picnic in Central Park. No
need for ferries.

The Roeblings' brainchild
Towers, girders, steel cables
Strung across the sky

ON VIEWING *BEHIND THE MYTH OF BENEVOLENCE*

—After Titus Kaphar

The model peers from behind a drape,
her face, one bare shoulder, one knee,
visible. Her only adornment, a turquoise
and gold headdress. Canvas folds
conceal most of her naked body,
reveal half a familiar likeness.

Viewers see a dark-complected woman,
stand-in for not only the light-complected
Sally Hemings, but other enslaved women
to whom personal choice was denied.

The artist affirms the portrait is—
and is not—about Sally and the master
of Monticello, a contradiction clear
to all who know the story of Jefferson
and the fair-skinned, but enslaved,
half-sister of his dead wife.

I take it all in, our country's history
with its shadow side, the homage to Peale's
neoclassicism, the artist's skillful depiction
of loose canvas falling from the plane.

Still what my eye returns to again and again
is the turban transported from Delft
to Virginia to crown a head bereft of pearls.

The Woman Who Refused

*But when the attendants delivered the king's
command, Queen Vashti refused to come.*

—Esther 1:12a

Xerxes was drunk, no other way to say it.
For six months, he strutted, bragged,
showed off his riches. For a full week,
he feasted and drank with princes
and soldiers. Wine was abundant
and the king imbibed freely.

No other way to say it, Xerxes was drunk
not only on spirits, but on greed and on pride.
He displayed silver, gold, linens
and pearls, gloated on envy in the eyes
of his nobles. That vain man craved more,
sent seven eunuchs to fetch *me*.

He sent seven eunuchs to bring one
more possession to stroke his own ego.
I was to enter wearing only my crown,
flaunt my face and my figure. I, Vashti,
was a king's wife, no man's concubine,
I was the queen and I would not come.

Whatever Dreams

We drove the rental car past the *Welcome*
to Las Vegas sign on our way to Zion
and Yellowstone. Past gold-clad towers,
lavish gardens, and fountains, the continuous
lines of people eager for photos
to show they made it.
We reached the north end of the strip.
Seedy, not glitzy. I saw her there.
She wasn't young and she wasn't old.
Her cheeks were sunken.
Lips closed over empty gums.
She pushed a grocery cart
piled with lumpy plastic bags.
Her hair was pulled into a ponytail,
blonde, but not flaxen like the towhead
she may have once been, nor golden
like a woman who keeps a standing
appointment with her stylist.
Her hair was the yellow of someone
who, whatever dreams had betrayed
her, still believed in them enough to buy
a bottle of peroxide at Rite Aid.

NOT JUST

It's not just poor water walkers
in Uganda, not just refugees
in camps far from home,
not only unhoused sleeping under bridges.
It's not just TV producers on assignment
with the anchor, or actors called back for an audition,
nor just the beautiful with glossy hair
and clear complexions nor the young
in tank tops and cutoff jeans.

It's children, runaways ensnared by traffickers,
women handed drinks at parties,
housewives bringing in the mail,
even great-grandmothers washing dishes.

Sisters, not one of us
is safe. Not one.

South Pacific

A girl collides with live theater
for the first time in Atlanta in 1952.

She is unaware Hammerstein and Rodgers
had firm intent their tunes proclaim love
for all. She does not know in New Haven
theatergoers suggested: *Cut that part*
and now Georgia legislators are railing
about half-breeds and praising
pure Southern blood.

She sits beside her mother mesmerized
by the spotlit stage.

She remembers Bloody Mary's
indignant accusation:
French planters stingy bastards!
then recalls her whispered question:
What's a bastard? and her mother's
reply: *Later.*

At home, the dictionary is no help.

Professor Laura Ellis Plays the Negro National Anthem from the University of Florida Bell Tower

Gainesville, Florida
October 19, 2017

Me, an activist? Good heavens, no.
I teach church music, the organ
and the carillon. Some say the bells
and pipes are passé. I disagree.

Twice each day, I trade my high-heel
pumps for trainers and with students,
climb the tower to peal the bells, flood
campus with notes, chords, melodies.

If I'm a zealot, my passion is music's
power to stir and soothe. When hate
marched in, I could not just grieve.
Recalling Florida's native son

who penned a song of liberty,
I mounted eleven flights,
roused bells to proclaim the anthem
James Weldon Johnson wrote

for schoolchildren to celebrate
the Great Emancipator.
Those boys and girls sang out
and kept on singing long after

Johnson journeyed north to join
the Harlem Renaissance. While
Richard Spencer spewed his bile,
"Lift Every Voice and Sing" rang out.

ODE TO THE SHAKER HYMN

Sing it anyhow, I said, when my daughter
quibbled it just wasn't seemly
for a wedding. I, the bride, if an old one,
and my groom, no younger, relished
the valley of love and delight, had grasped

gifts of being simple and free, found
them worth singing about. No matter
she could belt out "Ave Maria" without
rehearsal time. We knew the Shakers
told it true, at least about the place

just right. We couldn't buy the celibacy,
but oh, the tune, the melody. The music's
trek, England to Maine, Copland to Ma,
Graham's ballet, Crane's poem, Krauss's vocals,
all those variations mirrored our own long

separate journeys to simplicity, where
by turning we'd come round right. *Sing it!*

GEORGIA ON MY MIND

I mouth these sounds: *Hiawassee*, *Chattahoochee*,
Tallulah Falls,

    Add *Dahlonega*, *Senoia*, *Unicoi*. Stir in sweet gum,

camellia, Cherokee rose. Breathe in magnolia,
honeysuckle. Meditate

    on Antioch and Bethsaida, cemeteries where
    ancestors sleep.

Grandma rakes graves, arranges Aucuba in sturdy urns.

I name childhood teachers, Nellie Bean (who was mean),
Edith Ruff

    (who was gentle), Miss Jetta Dowis. I see the old
    granite church.

Rock of Ages. Baptismal waters close over me. When I rise,
sodden

    Choir robe hangs heavy. *Just As I Am, Without One Plea.*

I dream the dust of bicycle tires. See sisters and cousins.
Baskets

    cradle Mason jars with juice and hold peanut butter
    sandwiches.

We pedal a route then safe for children, now an interstate.
I see horses,

smell saddle and bridle, recall the leap from hayloft
to land

on sweet straw. Recollect the scolding for scattering
horses' feed.

I haunt red brick: College Street School, Hapeville Post
Office, our bungalow.

Picture Grandma's frame Victorian around the
corner, wisteria arbor

on one side, fish pond on the other. Out back a headless
chicken hangs

by its feet, later plucked at kitchen table. Half a block
away, the bakery,

chocolate eclairs, Cokes in six-ounce bottles.

I remember bus rides downtown to Atlanta. Buying
shoes at Thompson Boland Lee,

sliding feet into flouroscope, boney toes revealed.
Lunch at S&W. Rich's bridge

spans Forsyth Street. Car trips. Daddy drives, his
baritone belts *Chattanooga Choo*

Choo, croons *Carolina in the Morning*, booms *Caissons*
Rolling Along.

Mama's peach ice cream. Sprayberry's barbecue. Varsity
hot dogs.

I picture mimosa blossom powder puffs. Persimmons
rot on hot sidewalks. I hear

the whir of a June bug tethered to silk thread.
Chigger bites. Pal, the three-

legged dog next door. Outdoor play at dusk. *Red Rover*.
Simon Says. Lightning bugs

blink. Parents sit on porch steps, their cigarettes
glow red. Soft voices murmur.

About Tomatoes

Small as peas, they grew wild
in the Andes.

Aztecs cultivated, crossbred, cooked
them into sauces.

Conquistadors came hungry
for gold,

sailed home with a pennyweight
of tiny seeds.

In Italy, botanist Mattioli christened a new "eggplant,"
Pomo d'oro, "golden apples."

The fruit traveled to England, even Asia, before
diarist Salmon found shoots in South Carolina

where later my father relished homegrown
ones with his breakfast grits,

but only at season's peak, not, he swore,
when they tasted of cardboard.

My mother topped plates of fried sweet corn
with thick red slices of savory goodness.

For me, they are best with bacon and lettuce
in the trinitarian BLT.

The Question of Genesis

In the very beginning, God created all matter.
First formed skies above and farther below
made earth to exist as a shapeless splatter.
Next he shined light, set his formation aglow,

bisected night from day, parted waters, let appear
land, rooted some plants, yes, all vegetation,
fastened bright lights in the overhead sphere
to illumine day and night and be the causation

of days, year, and seasons. To seas, he assigned
fish, to the firmament sparrow, robin and wren,
to live on land he made the sheep and the hind.
In his own image, he fashioned women and men,

gave us the privilege of tending the garden.
Given the outcome, would he do it again?

Nameless

Four chapters in Judges tell Samson's
story: his father, Manoah, named
again and again; his mother, mentioned
only as *she*, *the woman*, *his wife*,
the once barren vessel by which Manoah
gained a son, one of those women
with closed wombs who inhabit pages
of the Bible, women like Sarah and Elizabeth,
too old to conceive, Rachel and Hannah,
who also yearned for children,
their rewards always sons,
no surprise conceptions
of daughters.

Jerusalem

Here on the eighth day Mary and Joseph took Jesus to temple
where the old prophet Simeon praised God for his promise,
rejoicing to see it fulfilled.

Here the Holy family celebrated Passover,
and their son questioned the teachers.

Here when a man cleansed the temple,
was greeted with palms and hosannas,
then mocked, beaten, crucified.

Here my friend, Elias, lives. Here his ancestors
have followed the way of Christ for centuries.

Today tourists shove to see where Jesus taught,
walk the Stations of the Cross on the Via Dolorosa,
buy crèches and crosses of olive wood.

Today Elias cannot vote, his papers claim no country.

Today he passes armed checkpoints to guide
pilgrims to Bethlehem and Jericho,
and back to Jerusalem.

Elias says, "I love this city. I hate this city."

Aphasia

We sit at her kitchen table
my sister and I
twenty years
since her stroke.

Her husband cooks using
both arms, both hands.
Later she'll wash dishes
her left arm,
left hand doing
the work
of two.

We talk the way we've learned.
She has something
to tell me, begins,
hesitates,
searches for
a phrase.

I wait, nod, supply a word now and then,
guess a little.
She spits out
part of her story.
We both exhale.

She catches my eye, laughs,

taps her forehead,
"There's so much
going on
in here."

I Don't Want to Be a Casino

—After "I Don't Want to Be a Spice Store"
   by Christian Wiman

I don't want to be a casino.

I don't want my rooms filled with slot machines

and blackjack tables.

I don't want to seduce grannies

to gamble away the grocery money

or to have my carpets reek of Lucky Strikes.

Casinos open too early and close

too late.

I want to be a bookshop where children find Magic Tree Houses

and Pippi Longstocking, where their mothers

can sit and rest.

I want shelves crammed with books arranged

alphabetically by authors' last names

or by topics like sorcery, history, art.

I hope to lure browsers with little white cards

naming "staff picks" in neat print

or loopy script,

to welcome readers with deep armchairs

and the smell of coffee. Maybe a cat
will sleep in the window.
Let me be a place where your biggest risk
will be rolling the dice
on a writer you've never read,
maybe Fredrik Backman,
J.R.R. Tolkien or Anne Lamott.
To up the ante.
To ante up.

Deficit Accounting

I'm not an acrobat. Not sliced okra
sizzling in hot grease, not a skinny cat
crouched beside the door. I'm not a brickbat
to be hurled at an amateur diva
just because she's singing off-key. I'm not
a hummingbird or a red-shouldered hawk
nor a schoolteacher's stubby piece of chalk,
not a sage philosopher's abstract thought.
No critic has called me silver-throated.
I go ignored in salons and saloons
so I stay home reading most afternoons.
No pizzazz here—I can't sugarcoat it—
fourteen lines illustrate things I am not.
As a novel, I'd live a juicier plot.

The Traveling Okra

"Okra is a Cinderella among vegetables."
Marjorie Kinnan Rawlings

—After Naomi Shihab Nye

Consider the lowly okra:
mucilaginous green pod
transported from West Africa

on slave ships. Stand and applaud
this unintentional offering
to Southern cuisine. Bend a knee

in praise of chunky bits fried
with fat saved from yesterday's
bacon. Or do as I do, chop

an onion, add tomatoes,
brown sugar, curry, make gumbo
from modest Cinderella.

Help her seduce the handsome prince.

DRUTHERS

You take the lobster Newberg,
beluga caviar, pheasant under glass.
They're not for me. I find my joy
in plainer fare. I'll make a BLT,
spread mayonnaise on soft, white
bread, add a crunchy strip of hickory
smoked, mate him with an Early Girl,
nestle the lovers on a counterpane
of iceberg lettuce.

For Those Who Bloom Late

She was a waif of a duckling exiled
by elements to hatch as surprise
in an alien nest. Hans's tale echoed

no lore bestowed by generations of Danes,
stole no saga from an ancient culture.
He wrote his own story.

His little bird was rebuffed all around
until a bevy of swans invited her
in. Swimming with them, she glimpsed

her own image there on the pond.
Why, I am as graceful as they.
Hans, gangly and tall, his nose far too long,

his feet far too big, loved drama and song.
Other lads teased him for not being like them.
I remember my own knobby knees

and stringy blond hair, awkward exchanges
when I hoped to be friends.

Some bloom early; they shine from the start.
Others are revealed upon reflection.

Me Too

1952

I am eleven.
My friend and I ride the city bus.
An unkempt man stares.
At her stop, my friend gets off.
I am now alone.
The stranger still stares.
I move to sit nearer the driver.
The creep slithers over, settles beside me, asks,
"Do you want to go to a movie?"
Eyes straight ahead, I croak
One word: "No."
At the next stop, I leap from the bus,
Run behind stores and through yards
Until I reach my own back door,
barrel inside where my mother
is calmly ironing.
I am home.

1981

I am forty,
On a business trip with colleagues.
I have a big presentation the next day.
After dinner the boss stands too close.
I walk away,

Scurry to my hotel room,
Get ready for bed,
Hear a knock. Through the closed door,
My boss invites, "Come out, have a brandy,
It'll settle your nerves." I decline, bolt the door.
I am angry.

2017

I am seventy-six.
Bold women speak out.
#MeToo trends.
I am reminded.

2024

I am eighty-three.
I write this poem.

That Sunday Morning

When she woke nothing hinted my mother
would slip from this world to the next by afternoon.

Skeletal after stroke, confined to wheelchair
and nursing home, she bore little resemblance

to the slender teenager who charmed older boys
at college cotillions. Nor to the wife who shimmied

her shapely hips when she and her husband danced
the Charleston — shocking their three daughters.

A small gasp — the only alarm — all it took
for one nurse to tell another: "She's dead."

When I arrived, Mother's mouth blazed as crimson
as *Bonfire*, the lipstick color she always wore

when she wanted to look her best. I blurted
"Who did the lipstick?"

"Miz Waters always wanted a little makeup
when we helped her dress."

No way to know she was about to make an exit,
but ready she was. Mother died with her lipstick on.

Open Casket

The pocket doors separating parlor
and dining room in my grandparents'
Victorian house are tucked away.
Huge arrangements of hothouse flowers

cover every surface. Funeral home
chairs line both rooms. The dining table
where we feast on Sundays (fried chicken,
rice and gravy, green beans, lemon pie),

is gone. An open casket rests on a bier
by the window. Summers, the arbor outside
glows lavender with wisteria. Today in January,
the bare vines display a starker beauty.
I am only five and a half, and I loved the man

whose body lies in the coffin. Mama lifts me
to see him one last time. Now that I'm old, I avoid
looking at the dead. *That's old-school*, I tell myself or
I'll remember her alive. Yet, this memory comforts.

I think of *Pops*, how kind he was, so at ease
with children, and of his pleated leather coin purse
flush with dimes for his grandchildren. I always
spent mine on éclairs at the bakery down the street.

CLEANING THE ALLEN FAMILY PLOT

We piled into the Jeep station wagon,
Mother at the wheel, Grandma, aunts, sisters,
cousins squeezed in. Bench seats without belts

and the open wayback gave room for all.
We carried rakes, brooms, Mason jars filled

with water and Aucuba cut from Grandma's yard.
We rumbled along a rural road, turned off to reach
Bethsaida Baptist Church where Grandfather—

our Pops—was buried. His death
was fairly recent then; I see that now.

His wife's and daughters' sadness must have
been still fresh. We girls paid grief no mind,
bounded around the country churchyard,

reading names and dates on tombstones,
tormenting June bugs, scratching chigger bites.

What gave an eerie feeling was Grandma's name
already chiseled next to his on the double
grave marker when she was still right there,

alive, raking winter's accumulation
of curled-up leaves.

To My Ancestors

"As long as there is one person on Earth who remembers you,
it isn't over."

—Oscar Hammerstein

I looked in courthouses,
archives, graveyards,
hefted huge (and dusty)
record books, scrolled
grainy reels of microfilm,
climbed over barbed wire
fences, all in hope I'd find you,
document each and every life.

I read censuses, deeds, wills,
inventories and shouted
hallelujah for every forebear
found. When the light came
on, I understood reality.
Each father discovered, every
mother located would also
have two parents.

That's more two more
ancestors to search out,
two more stories to flesh out.
The quest is never-ending.
Still, in thanks for life you gave me,
I'm game to carry on.

Acknowledgments

I am grateful to my longtime poetry sisters—Jane Mary Curran, Karen Luke Jackson, and Emily Wilmer—whose kind and insightful comments helped improve many of these poems. Their friendship and encouragement belie the idea that writing is always a solitary pursuit.

Ken Chamlee has been my teacher, my mentor, and my friend. His suggestions for revisions and ordering have benefited this collection immensely.

Although I no longer live near enough to participate in classes as part of The Great Smokies Writing Program, I am still a fan of this unique program for writers in many genres. Any poetic skill I have achieved is due to sitting at the feet of stellar teachers such as Cathy Smith Bowers, Ken Chamlee, Tina Barr, and Eric Nelson and alongside gifted classmates.

I thank the editors of journals and anthologies who selected many of these poems for publication, sometimes in earlier versions:

After
"I Don't Want to Be a Casino"

Celestial Musings: Poems Inspired by the Night Sky
"I Did Not Learn the Stars"

Christian Feminism Today, Untold Volumes:
"Nameless" · "The Woman Who Refused"

Delta Poetry Review
"The Old Smith Place" · "Time Suspended"

The Ekphrastic Review
"Urban Altarpiece"

Kakalak
"Cleaning the Allen Family Plot" · "Deficit Accounting" ·
"Druthers" · "For Those Who Bloom Late" · "Gathering
the Flocks" · "Mortality" · "Ode to the Shaker Hymn" ·
"On Viewing *Behind the Myth of Benevolence*" ·
"The Traveling Onion" · "Whatever Dreams"

Minnow
"Sulphur Springs Loop, Paris Mountain State Park"

The Power of the Feminine I (Volume II)
"Professor Laura Ellis Plays the Negro National
Anthem from the University of Florida Bell Tower"

The Rose in the World
"The Question of Genesis"

Salvation South
"About Tomatoes" · "Along the Laurel River Trail" ·
"A Busy Intersection in Savannah" · "Cypress Knees" ·
"Georgia on My Mind" · "Gorges State Park" · "Mess?
What Mess?" · "A Walk Around Lake Mayer"

Immense thanks are due to publisher and editor Leigh E. Rich for carving out time from her numerous and varied responsibilities to shepherd this collection to completion.

Finally, I am blessed to share life with my husband, James "Jim" Green. Having him as partner and friend has led to, among many exciting things, the hiking poems in this book.

About the Author

© Landon Westbrook

Born in South Carolina, Anne Waters Green
is a poet who has spent much of her life in
Georgia and recently returned to Savannah
after fifteen years in western North Carolina.

She is the author of the chapbooks *The Season
Lengthens* and *Minute Men and Women*.

Her poems also have appeared in *Kakalak*,
The Great Smokies Review, *Christian Feminism
Today*, *Delta Poetry Review*, *Salvation South*,
and other journals and anthologies.

monte ceceri

In the early 1500s, it was from the heights of Monte Ceceri — otherwise known as "Swan Mountain" — in Fiesole, Italy, that inventor and artist Leonardo da Vinci let soar one of his experimental flying machines.

Envisioning a future where such fantastical creations would one day become reality, Leonardo desired to fill the world with awe-inspiring inventions and ideas.

Like its namesake's Renaissance roots, Monte Ceceri Publishers supports avant-garde writers whose works challenge current perspectives, inspire new paths, and speak to a modern-day humanism.

Based in Savannah, Georgia, Monte Ceceri is an independent publisher of books that raise issues of social, cultural, and philosophical interest, cross disciplinary boundaries, and facilitate cross-cultural dialogue through effective and engaging writing.

SwanHorse Press is an imprint of
Monte Ceceri Publishers, LLC

www.ingramcontent.com/pod-product-compliance
Lightning Source LLC
Chambersburg PA
CBHW022105020426
42335CB00012B/833